The Consummate Professional's Guide to Referral Marketing

Or:

How to maximise your professional credibility, status and success

By:
Vince Golder
Steve Mullins

Published by New Generation Publishing in 2018

Copyright © Vince Golder
& Steve Mullins 2015

First Edition

The author asserts the moral right under the Copyright, Designs and Patents Act 1988 to be identified as the author of this work.

All Rights reserved. No part of this publication may be reproduced, stored in a retrieval system or transmitted, in any form or by any means without the prior consent of the author, nor be otherwise circulated in any form of binding or cover other than that in which it is published and without a similar condition being imposed on the subsequent purchaser.

ISBN: 978-1-78955-339-0

www.newgeneration-publishing.com

The Consummate Professional's Guide to Referral Marketing

How to maximise your professional credibility, status and success

As pressures increase on each of us to compete more strongly for jobs, sales or promotion it becomes ever more important to present well and relate well, because given the choice of two people with similar credentials the one who comes over more professionally will almost certainly be the winner.

This short book words is written for the decision-makers and influencers in organisations, whether profit driven or not-for-profit.

The aim is to help you do better personally and to help your organisations thrive, whatever your walk of life or stakeholders' expectations.

By:
Vince Golder
Steve Mullins

Enjoy

Contents:

Some Thank-Yous 1
Maximise Your Professional Credibility 3
  About the book 3
  Disclaimer 5
Part 1. The Consummate Professional 7
  Introduction 9
  Section 1: The Independent Professional ... 11
    1.1. Credibility 11
    Table 1. Where the Specialist Scores 13
    1.2. Why businesses hire Independents 14
      1,2.1. Finding the right professional: 14
      1.2.2. What are you worth as a professional? . 15
    Table 2. Self-appraisal – find your PQ. 16
  Section 2: About You 18
  Section 3: Your Approach 20
  Section 4: Assets and Hidden Assets 23
  Section 5: Personal Relationships 25
  Section 6: Client relationships 29
  Section 7: Feedback and Follow-on 32
  Section 8: Client Review Meetings 34
    8.1. The Aims 34
    8.2. The Process 35
    8.3. Review Meeting – Points to Cover 35
    8.4. Review Meetings - In Conclusion 37
  Section 9: Developing your business 38
    9.1. Be a Brutal Pragmatist 38
    9.2. Empathy 40
    9.3. Work to Your Strengths – Niche Marketing 41
    9.4. Client Focus and Commitment 43
    9.5. Relationship Communication 44
    9.6. Work Hard but Maintain Perspective 46
    9.7. A note about Referral Marketing 47

Section 10: Why People Refer You 48
10.1. Types of Referrals 48
10.1.1. Relationship Referrals 48
10.1.2. Transaction Based Referrals.............. 49
10.1.3. Your Referral Marketing Programme... 50
10.2. Joint Venture or Alliance Marketing........ 53
10.2.1. A Joint Venture Model 54
10.2.2. The Potential Benefits of Joint Venture 55
10.2.3. Examples of Joint Venture Marketing.. 57

Part 2. Business Networking 61
Introduction 63

Your Networking Plan 63
General Principles 63
At the reception 64
In General 66
Introductions... 67
Conversations.. 67
Asking Questions 68
Remembering Names 69
Business Cards 69
Body Language.. 70
The Graceful Exit 70
Follow-up... 71

Types of Meeting.. 72
Breakfast meetings 72
Open Networking Groups 72
People who Lunch 73
Unstructured Networking.............................. 74
Specialist Groups 74
Business Forums... 75
Virtual Networking 76

Tip of the Week... 76
Example Tip of the week 77

Part 3. Referral Marketing 79
Introduction 81
Section A - Maximise Your Referrals 82
A1. 24 tips 82
A2. Givers' Gain 86
A3. Business Networking 87
Section B - Generate More Sales 88
B1. Ensure Employee Engagement.................. 88
B2. Strategic Customer Care (SCC)................. 90
B3. Grow business through your customers..... 93
B4. Differentiate your Offering 94
B5. Campaign Tactics 96
B6. Niche Marketing 99
B7. Value for Money (VFM) 101
B8. Some sales truisms............................... 102
Section C. - More Referral Marketing 106
C1. The Power of Referral Marketing 106
C2. Why Referral Marketing Works............... 109
In Conclusion 113
Services 114
To contact Vince Golder: 114
About the Contributors 115
Terms of Use and Disclaimers 117
Other Related Publications 120
Books.. 120
Articles 120
Papers 121

Some Thank-Yous

The real people to thank are the Owner Managers and corporate decision-makers who have embraced the techniques and approaches described here in their organisations.

Not only has their enthusiasm benefited many hundreds of organisations but also provided many years of experience to weed, prune and nourish the original material in order to get to the stuff that really matters.

To those people with the drive, courage and desire to win – a heartfelt *Thank You*

Maximise Your Professional Credibility

About the book

Referral marketing works as well for people as it does for organisations, this is because it is based on:

Presentation: Showing best reasons as to why someone should do business with you or refer you, or to employ you

Relationship: Developing the best relationship with customers, contacts, work colleagues, family, friends etc. Great relationships will maximise goodwill, appreciation, loyalty, satisfaction, referrals, promotion and quality of personal life

Planning: Operating a structured, systematic and strategic plan that will increase the success of your professional and business career.

This handy book draws together the many years experience Vince has enjoyed as a coach, strategist, salesman and marketer in supporting businesses in improving their sales, marketing and profitability.

In an increasingly busy world we have tried to make every sentence count, eliminate padding and produce a pocket book that is both a guide and a point of easy reference.

There are three sections:

Become the Consummate Professional
You will consider a range of tips, exercises and practical experience to help you present yourself in the best possible light in a range of business settings.

Business Networking
Built on the best possible you, we explore how to reach out to other business people to grow your professional circle and credibility in the most effective manner.

Referral Marketing
With sound interpersonal skills and a network of fellow professionals, we finally look at how to develop increasing volumes of business from referrals, which experts believe will be over 70% of the route to market within a few years.

Please go back over material from time to time, experiment, find what works best for you and enjoy increasing success, both personally and for your organisation

Disclaimer

Any reference to fees paid are for example purposes only or quoted from recognised sources and do not represent any potential fees you can earn as an independent professional.

Whilst this book has been written to help you to achieve your desired business and revenue goals, the results of such goals are totally dependent on your own efforts and commitment in the implementation of your business and not the responsibly of the authors of this publication in any way.

Part 1. The Consummate Professional

Introduction

This book is for:
- The independent professional
- The person contemplating becoming independent
- The executive sales person
- All managers, executives and senior directors

Being professional is not just looking smart and acting in an efficient manner, there are many additional factors that make the consummate professional and the more of these factors you can incorporate in your professional being, the greater success you will have in your career or business.

The book is in a quick reference format for easier reading and ready reference; it has been complied with the contribution of successful professionals with many years experience, who have been there and done it, made the mistakes, learnt the lessons and achieved the rewards to be enjoyed from conducting themselves in the best professional manner.

The model we have used follows a number of stages:
– Looking and acting professionally.
– What it is that makes you special.
– Reasons why people should do business with you.
– Delivering customer benefit.

- Adding value to your professional services and worth.
- Developing your business.

We suggest you read this book several times; the first time to use it as a questionnaire to explore your own current professional rating and subsequent readings to develop a business model that is right for you.

Consider each subject honestly as to how it applies to you e.g. "are you a good listener?" Your answer might be "I must admit I don't always listen that well and tend to talk too much". If you know your own mistakes and can rectify them, then you can gain an increasingly higher professional standing.

We believe we have included good coverage of the many important factors needed to be the consummate independent professional; if you think we have missed anything please contact us with your suggestions and, as appropriate, we will add them to the book and give you full recognition for them. We would also welcome your feedback on the book and the help it has given you in developing your career.

Here's to your future professional and business success.

Section 1: The Independent Professional

1.1. Credibility

Anyone can print a few business cards to claim to be an Independent Professional and, unfortunately, there are many such cowboys out there giving the profession a bad name. Please check the credentials of anyone providing professional advice, we offer a couple of tables on professional qualities in this publication.

The true Independent Professional is an independent contractor who has specialist knowledge, experience and expertise in a particular field or sector, who can improve your organisation in a number of ways, including: solving problems, get a tricky job done, make processes more efficient, create new wealth, or save money. Good Independent Professionals work to a negotiated contract or agreement.

When taking on a Independent Professional, business owners have the availability of someone who is outside their company and can bring a range of benefits, both immediate and in the longer term, for example:
- To see the bigger picture
- To provide wider skills not available in house
- To bring additional experience,
- To add new contacts,
- To have the nerve to challenge accepted wisdom

- To coach or mentor people whilst any changes are being implemented.

There are many advantages with taking on the Independent Professional and few risks; a good quote I once heard went "A great Independent Professional can reinvent the wheel for you".

A calculation that includes items such as holiday pay, NIC, secretarial costs for example shows that the hired professional will actually save money, there's an example facing.

Please contact the author if you require a more detailed breakdown for your organisation.

Table 1. Where the Specialist Scores

How hiring a specialist can deliver financial benefits as well as technical ones

A comparison between salaried staff and the Independent Professional

Attribute	Staff	Cost	Professional	Cost	Difference
Specialist skills	Maybe	-	Yes	-	
Bound by protocol	Yes	-	No	-	+
Backed by experts	No	-	Yes	-	+
Paid by results	No	-	Yes	-	+
Good with change	Maybe	-	Yes	-	
Client Charter	No	-	Yes	-	+
Hidden agenda	Probably	-	No	-	+
Constructive criticality	Unlikely	-	Yes	-	
Alternative approach	Unlikely	-	Yes	-	
Experience of competitors	Unlikely	-	Yes	-	
Hours worked	Fixed + O/T	-	Flexible	-	
Hard to remove	Yes	-	No	-	+
Cost to replace (avge.)		£13,000		Nil	+
Annual salary (avge.)		£50,000		£68,000	£(18,000)
Employer's NI		£5,000		Nil	£5,000
Pension – emp. contribution		£1,000		Nil	£1,000
O/T, bonuses etc.		£5,000		Nil	£5,000
BUPA		£250		Nil	£250
Car & Expenses		£7,500		Nil	£7,500
Training & CPD		£1,000		Nil	£1,000
PA & secretarial		£2,000		Nil	£2,000
				Total financial benefit	**£3,750**

Annual salary is based on:

A staff member working 210 days per year (losing: 104 days as weekends, 30 days holiday, 12 days sick and 9 days public holidays) – equivalent to £240 per day.

An Independent Professional charging £650 per day but typically only active on the project for 2 days per week – equivalent to £68,000 per annum.

<u>1.2. Why businesses hire Independents</u>

– For their specialist skills, knowledge, experience and being team players.
– They are a cost effective, practical and risk free option (please see the Comparison Chart two pages on).
– Independent Professionals can help improve turnover.
– They can save businesses money, often quickly enough to start covering their fees.

1,2.1. Finding the right professional:

Sticking a pin in Yellow Pages or using an on-line search engine will often unearth the best presented, not necessarily the most capable or appropriate to your circumstances.

Generally finding the right Independent Professional for the job will involve word of mouth introductions.

Good Independent Professionals come with good references, testimonials and case studies where they have actually participated in delivering the best solutions.

1.2.2. What are you worth as a professional?

It is very important to know what benefits and value you bring to potential clients so that you can clearly present your worth and demonstrate why clients should hire you and to justify the fees you require.

The best way you can present this is to use testimonials and case studies from previous clients, preferably with details of what you have achieved; here are a few examples:

– Increased ABC Industries annual profit margin by 10% resulting in an additional £1m p.a.

– Increased Jasons Electrical productivity by 20%

– Reduced operating costs for Daltons Distribution by 30% resulting in a saving of £50,000 p.a.

Table 2. Self-appraisal – find your PQ.

Rate your own Professionalism Quotient (1 – very weak; 10 – very strong)

	Selected Qualities	Your rating out of 10	Weighting	Score Rate x Wt.
1.	You look, act, present and work as a professional		8	
2.	You have a genuine interest in people		7	
3.	You readily develop lasting relationships		9	
4.	You are a good listener		9	
5.	You are easily understood		8	
6.	You are adaptive and flexible		7	
7.	Your presentation material looks good and feels good		6	
8.	You constantly look for referral opportunities		5	
9.	You give more referrals than you receive		8	
10	You spend time to be confident of client needs		9	
11	You collect referrals and testimonials		5	
12	You don't offer financial discounts		5	
13	You actively challenge the client's accepted wisdom		6	
14	You have a high level of trust and credibility		9	
15	You regularly hold review meetings with the client		6	
16	You always check the job is completed satisfactorily		9	
17	You always ask if more can be done		8	
18	You provide the client with referrals		6	
19	You can readily call on other specialists		7	
20	You are comfortable with change		5	

21	You have a Customer Charter		8	
22	You have a proven track record of success		7	
23	You publish, blog or deliver webinars		5	
24	You have awards for your achievements		6	
25	You are a member of a professional association		7	
			Your total	

Multiply your score by 100 = _____, then

Divide your multiplied score by 1,750 = _____%

This is your **Professionalism Quotient**

Section 2: About You

People do business with people and the most valuable asset in your business is yourself. The more presentable, knowledgeable and helpful you are, and the more benefits and value you give, the more people will be attracted to do business with you.

A true professional never stops trying to improve themselves, both personally and on a business basis to maintain the highest standards and commercial potential.

Your Initial Contact with people should consider:

1. – **Presentation,** always be smartly dressed, clean, tidy and well groomed, no matter what your professional outfit, be it a suit, casual dress or overalls.

2. – **Manner**, SMILE, give a firm (not crushing) handshake, give a pleasant and SINCERE greeting.

3. – **Be Confident**, remember you are the expert in your field and you will know much more than the prospect / client, so be confident in all your presentations, dealings, advice, consultancy or coaching role.

4. – **Attitude**, Your attitude is THE MOST IMPORTANT quality you have to make you the consummate professional.

You MUST have a great attitude in two areas:
- A constructive attitude that enables you to find solutions to the challenges and situations presented.
- A positive attitude to people that makes you helpful, patient, with good understanding and friendly towards everyone you meet and work with.

5. – *Be genuinely interested* in the people you meet, establish good eye contact, but don't stare them out, be sincerely interested in what they talking about, listen, ask questions to get them talking.

6. – *Develop lasting relationships* naturally, Top Professionals know that long-term, positive relationships set the groundwork for new sales, repeat sales, increased client satisfaction and loyalty and – importantly future referrals.

7. – *DO NOT BE ARROGANT* thinking: "I'm the expert. I'm going to tell them what to do, submit my bill, and be on my way." This almost never works. That's because even familiar business situations can vary greatly from place to place.

Section 3: Your Approach

8. – *Be a great listener*, the first and most essential part of communication is listening and acting on the information you are given. An Independent Professional with excellent communications skills spends their first hour or two - or even a day or two - asking questions and listening carefully to answers.

Only after the Independent Professional has taken in a great deal of information from the client will they be ready to understand how their own expertise can be best applied to the situation to get the job done.

Never forget you have 2 ears and one mouth, use them in that order and proportion.

9. – *Before* you give ANY advice, make sure you fully understand the client's business, industry and their specific needs.

10. – *Have an easy and fluid skill* of imparting your knowledge and understanding to others and in a way that they can easily pick up what they are told and how to apply it.

11. – *Be adaptable and flexible*, most Independent Professionals have the experience of working in various industries, so they need to be adaptive because they will often find themselves in a unique situation with the client.

Each client's business is different and has to be treated in an individual way, so a good Independent Professional adapts.

Differences can include: variations in business models, the manager's own perspective, the expectations of shareholders and even the expectations of the Independent Professional can differ from client to client.

12. – *Never ever waffle*, always speak clearly and truthfully and never tell lies, or try and cover up that you cannot answer a question, or that pretend you know more than you do.

For awkward questions and situations where you do not have a suitable and immediate answer say something like "That is a good question I would like take a little time to look into the best answer for you and get back by ………………".

13. – *Avoid slang, acronyms and jargon*, it is essential you speak to clients clearly so that they fully understand you, and you understand them.

14. – *Do not appear desperate* and chase prospects too hard, People will soon know if you are desperate for business and will either not take you on, or take advantage of you.

If a prospect is giving you too much hassle on your fee rate or working arrangements, then do not hesitate to drop them and find a better prospect.

Such people are not worth dealing with and will cause problems you can well do without – both now and in the future.

Easier said than done though!

Section 4: Assets and Hidden Assets

15. - *A successful background* – success breeds success. Given a well documented and proven history and background of a person who has consistently done well and delivered professionally, continually deepens your credibility.

16. - *Your current skills and future development*. To be an effective Independent Professional and bring value to your clients and justification for your fees, you must be fully qualified with the level of skills required to achieve your role successfully.

Be thorough in your ongoing skill and Continuing Professional Development and take whatever training you can on subjects that will complement the services you provide. You can use additional skills and qualifications in your presentations and as you become more in demand you can ask for higher fees based on your wider knowledge and expertise.

17. - *Professional presentation – your materials*, some of the things to consider include:
– Only use professional high quality business cards
– Professional presentation packs
– An excellent website
– An e-mail address that incorporate your business name (not Hotmail for example).

- Produce good quality PowerPoint presentations
- Ensure there are no typos in any presentation

18. – ***Reputation***, when you embody the right qualities, you will develop a great reputation which is something that gets broadcast far and wide; it is one of the most valuable assets of a top professional.

19. – ***Have a referral mind-set***, all the most successful Independent Professionals gain much of their business through word of mouth referrals from their clients and business contacts – and at nil cost. This powerful means of lead generation used in a structured and systematic manner is called Referral Marketing. Its effectiveness is dependent on your own mind set and strategic approach, but more about referral marketing later.

20. – ***Remember*** the other often overlooked assets in your business: these include: your clients who apart from paying your wages are the referral sales force in your business, your partners, associates, employees, industry contacts, peers and also alliance partners.

Section 5: Personal Relationships

The difference between success and failure as an independent professional in all fields is generally down to having the right positive approach and good attitude to people.

Some of the elements that support personal success are:

21. – **Your first impression**, most people form lasting judgments during the first 10-20 seconds of meeting a new person. Ensure your first impression to existing clients or new prospects is exemplary, and continually work on how you can improve the first impression you give.

Some people have described this as <u>the four 15s</u>:
- An initial judgement is normally from 15 feet away,
- Firming up on that judgement with your top 15 inches (head and shoulders),
- Confirming that judgement within 15 seconds of you speaking, and if you don't make the right impression,
- It will take you at least 15 minutes to recover the situation.

22. – **Be very confident**, No apologies for repeating this.

23. – **Listen**, to the client, gain an emotional impression as well as using your ears more than your mouth. No apologies for repeating this either.

24. – ***Always determine the needs*** of the client and their contacts, ask enough (but not too many) questions to fully understand their issues, concerns, constraints and desires. Use open questions – what, where, why, when, who and how.

25. – ***Quick (but not glib) problem solving*** and issue handling – Clients put an extremely high value on business people who they know can solve problems and sort out complex situations quickly and easily to their satisfaction and in a practical and actionable manner.

26. – ***Be Client Focused***, Having a client focus is a strong contributor to the overall success of any business and involves ensuring that all aspects of the company put its clients' satisfaction first. Also, having a client focus includes maintaining an effective and structured client relations and service programme.

27. – ***Availability,*** ensure that you are always easily contactable, and reply quickly. Reply to all phone calls and emails at the very first opportunity and where possible use a live answering service.

28. – ***Client Charter*** – Providing your own Client Charter to prospects shows that you are truly client focused and demonstrates the best professional practice.

It's also tangible proof that you care about clients and how you will serve them.

Present your client charter where possible, for example on your website, proposals, profile, marketing media and even on the back of your invoices. This charter should be a maximum of one page and can include, but is not restricted to:
- Your Mission statement or Pledge – the commitment and standards you provide
- Policy regarding fees and payment terms (optional),
- Client care and aftercare
- Complaints procedure,
- Referral policy and expectation to be referred
- Guarantees and how they will be met

It is our experience that having and presenting a professional client charter can be a deciding factor in winning business and it does present you as the ultimate professional to a prospective client or contact.

29. – **Written instructions**; It's a big plus if an Independent Professional can provide written instructions that are easy to read in addition to good verbal communications. Being able to provide and leave written instruction behind for your clients multiplies your value enormously.

As a general rule competency in both oral and written skills greatly enhance the value of an Independent Professional.

30. – ***Do not offer financial discounts***, you know what you are worth and the benefits and value you can provide to a client, so do not discount your services or products unless it is to:
- Use a special offer on one small sale to attract a new client on a bigger contract.
- To make an up-sale with an existing client.
- To best use your time during a known quite period.

If a discount will secure a job with more to follow, don't offer money, perhaps offer three days for two – at your full charge-out rate, which will then be held for the follow-on work where there is no discount expected and no tricky negotiations to get your price back to where it should be.

Section 6: Client relationships

31. - *Bring a fresh perspective*, Companies often need a fresh set of eyes and ideas and it's astonishing at the amount of value Independent Professionals can add based on the most routine observations and insights.

Some may state that this is an example of Independent Professionals selling hyped common sense, but it can be easy for a company's staff to work in daily routines without a critical eye looking towards improved efficiency, effectiveness and improvement.

I have made many of these observations with my own clients; one example was my suggestion to an IT client with an IT training department. This department used over 40 phone lines to their training computers linked to an outside server.

I suggested to get rid of their many phone lines and instead have all their incoming calls channelled through an existing fibre optic line from their HQ building, an idea which saved the client £30,000 on their annual phone bill.

Now I'm not an IT professional and they were, yet it made sense to me and this saving paid for a good part of my annual fee.

32. - *Offer options*, present the client with a choice of possible solutions. If none of those choices meet the client's needs, reassure the client that you wish to continue to help them as best as you can and ask for time to gather more information to broaden or narrow the search for a more suitable solution.

33. – *Trust, credibility, integrity, reliability* – These are the qualities your clients must see in you. They will only see them if you truly have them! Such attributes are extremely difficult to fake.

34. – *Quality of products and service*, the quality of your product and service is a direct reflection on you. When people like you, trust you and admire your reputation, they will keep coming back and making referrals.

35. – *Communication with clients*, the more a client thinks positively about you and your business the better the relationship you will have and the more referrals you will receive. Regular, meaningful and practical communications between you and your client are essential yet must be finely balanced and not intrusive.

36. – *Treat clients appropriately*, don't just treat your clients as you would like to be treated, treat them EVEN BETTER than you would like to be treated.

37. – *Call to Action*: Have a clear call to action plan of what to do next, be it to: make a call, have a meeting, or make a decision by a certain time. Be firm on this as it is your role is to guide them and not the other way round.

38. – *Do not send an important proposal*
or quote by email or post, ALWAYS present it in person for best impact, to answer important questions and to close the deal. You will greatly increase your sales closure success if you do.
If prospects insist you send proposals to them first, I would suggest you politely decline stating:
"Your proposal is important and I'd hate to see it missed or lost, therefore I would much prefer to present it personally".

Later can be added *"in that way I can answer queries as they crop up, not leave them unresolved."*

Care: It has been my experience that prospects wanting proposals sent to them are often likely to give your ideas to a competitor who has already been selected, or to take your good ideas for free because they've decided to do the job themselves.

Section 7: Feedback and Follow-on

39. – ***Thank your clients for their business***. The client's time is valuable whether they spent money with you or not; thank them for contacting, visiting, or doing business with you and provide the means for them to welcome you back. Consider sending them a "Thank You for Your Business" letter normally at the end of the year.

40. – ***Ask clients how satisfied they are***, whether you have been able to provide the exact product or service the client wants or not; they must be satisfied that you have done your best to understand them and their needs, treated them with courtesy and respect and provided them with the best solution currently available.

41. – ***Check if there is any more you can do***, whether or not you have been able to satisfy the client's initial problem, look for ways to provide additional products or services to ensure that the client has had a good experience.

42. – ***Referrals and testimonials,*** when people have purchased your products or services, check that they were very satisfied, and then enquire if they know of anyone else who might like to enjoy the same benefits as they have received.

If clients are very happy, ask them for testimonials – if they are unsure what to write, write it for them! and be sure to get them to sign it and date it.

43. – **Provide closure,** afterwards ask if you can provide additional service and if the client is fully satisfied, close the sale and leave open the means to return, thank them and say a pleasant goodbye. Follow up with your client communication programme – see later.

44. – **If possible, add further value** to your client, for example:
- By providing referrals to potential Business to Business customers.
- By introducing other top Independent Professionals or businesses from your Alliance Group who can help them in other areas of their business.
- By training key staff to take over some of your role in the long-term.
- By providing free business workshops for your client and client's customers where you speak on your specialist subject – an excellent goodwill gesture from your client to their customers and a great opportunity for you to present yourself to future prospects.

You can make the workshop more varied if you invite other Independent Professionals who specialise in other business skills as guest speakers.

Section 8: Client Review Meetings

The Client Review Meeting Process is a high standard professional interview to maximise the quality and extra value of the business service and the relationship you provide to your client and it opens further long-term opportunities for you.

Review Meetings can be held at any time, especially at a crucial juncture in a project. Good seasonal times to establish continuity of work with clients are September when annual returns are being considered and January when most companies are thinking about their business plans for the coming financial year.

8.1. The Aims

The aims of review meetings should include getting up to date with:

- The results of the work you have done so far for the client, what your clients think about you, the level of their satisfaction and whether you have successfully met agreed targets to date.

- To agree and reinforce the benefits and value you have provided and to correct any issues or misunderstandings.

- What your clients want for their business and what they are planning to do for the future and the likely challenges.

- How you will help them to find the best solutions to these challenges through your own efforts and appropriate contacts from your professional network.

-To gain further goodwill with your clients by referring them to potential Business-to-Business customers.

-To gain client referrals, testimonials and case studies for yourself.

8.2. The Process

- Inform the client that the review meeting is very important, all main company decision makers are to attend and the meeting must not be disturbed.

- All review meetings MUST BE WELL PLANNED with a clear agenda sent to all participants well ahead of time.

- Present your review meeting process to every new prospect and existing clients clearly, why you conduct them and the benefit and value they give to clients.

8.3. Review Meeting – Points to Cover

- Relevant questions as to the results and performance of your own services/products, their level of satisfaction, any issues or ideas and record feedback.

- Ask them questions about their business i.e.

what are ALL their challenges, are they wanting to expand, are they seeking certain suppliers, do they have any staff problems.

- When they open up to you, note their key issues, buzz words and touch points.

- If you are a member of a professional Joint Venture group then give a brief announcement of your association with that group, use their own key words back to them and state confidently that you and your partners can fully meet their various challenges.

- On completion of the needs analysis you can offer to introduce them to the appropriate partners in your Joint Venture group with the relative skills that can solve their challenges.

- Offer to refer them FIRST (if you are happy to) and gain details of their required contacts.

- You pass on client's details to all appropriate partners who will contact the client at the first opportunity.

- If you and your client are happy to do so, you can ask your Joint Venture partners to help find your client's referral requests to potential contacts – this adds a great deal of goodwill, benefit and value for each partner.

- Ask them for testimonials and referrals for you in an indirect manner.

8.4. Review Meetings - In Conclusion

The Review Meeting Process is a very powerful means of adding great value at minimal cost to you, it creates long-term business, maximises customer satisfaction, gains valuable testimonials and opens the way to additional referred business.

However, as with all professional processes it only works well if you plan and operate it to a very high standard.

Conducting a client review meeting process will provide a successful continuation and potential additional growth to your sales and business.

Section 9: Developing your business

9.1. Be a Brutal Pragmatist

You will sometimes find yourself in a difficult situation when meeting a new client, who may be excited about a particular project or course of action which, from experience, you recognize as potentially disastrous.

The client is so excited about the project, that the last thing they want is someone pouring cold water on it. Rather, they seek yet another yes man who will join the team and help put the plan in action.

The dilemma for the Independent Professional is this: Does he or she tell the client what they want to hear, or steer them towards the brutal truth. It's a dilemma because the Independent Professional is in a position to make a lot of money if he or she simply tells the client what they want to hear, tell them they have a great idea, and gets to work on the project.

After the job is done, the Independent Professional can walk away with a nice fee, but what happens when the project results in disaster a short while later? The Independent Professional gets blamed and their reputation is damaged; if they have a Client Charter a great deal of time could be spent in rectification and consequential loss of potential future business.

It's far better to be honest and brutally frank when your gut and experience dictates it.

Some clients will be hell-bent on committing economic suicide. The best you can do is to talk them out of it. Give them your best advice. If they don't listen, you at least don't have to go down with their ship.

It can be a tough decision. It's very hard for any self-employed Independent Professional to turn down a consultancy fee, but sometimes you have to for your own sake and that of the client who could have been.

It could turn out that the client goes ahead with another Independent Professional who does take the money and run and when the project is a failure, the client will remember your advice, concerns and reluctance to work with them and will respect you for it and may even come back to you.

It wouldn't do you any harm to follow up on them to check out how their project went, if a failure then you could still have an opportunity to help them out and this time they will listen to you – and pay a higher fee to be rescued.

A Word of Warning: If all else fails with trying to correct the situation, then it would be very advisable to issue the client with a written statement which details your concerns and possible outcome.

This action puts your side of the situation on

record and covers you if the client persists to continue with their ideas. If there is a negative outcome from the client's ideas then you are fully covered and you would have done your job in advising the client from pursuing a weak idea.

Working Agreement: Always get clients to sign an official working agreement that clearly specifies the required result, how you work and also what is expected of the client. Such a document should present a clear overview of what is expected by all parties and clearly state the expected outcome.

<u>9.2. Empathy</u>

When most business owners are asked what they want from an Independent Professional, often highest on the list is: "To be understood."

People hire Independent Professionals when they have a situation they can't comfortably handle themselves, or with their own internal resources. Very often, business owners feel they have problems or needs that only they understand.

When they bring in an outside Independent Professional, they are extremely eager to explain their situation and needs in order to be understood; this is where being a great listener is vital.

Great Independent Professionals go out of

their way to properly understand a situation in context; they go beyond acknowledging the situation to understanding and establishing true empathy with their clients.

Empathy is described in the dictionary as: Identification with, and understanding of, another's situation, feelings and motives.

Empathy is important. It helps you understand the motivations and emotions of your client, not just the practical aspects of the operation.

The best Independent Professional recommendations take all aspects into account. A detached yet empathetic Independent Professional can give reasonable advice that is in the client's best interests - whether the client likes it or not. You can't force a client to do what you recommend, but you always have to try.

9.3. Work to Your Strengths – Niche Marketing

Maximise your business potential – narrow your marketing focus

A niche market is defined by many factors which include size, geographical location, buying requirements, specific needs, type of business, culture, age groups and gender to name a few.

Seriously consider adapting your skills to one or more very narrow niche markets as this approach will greatly increase your success.

Independent Professionals who offer niche services and market enjoy a much higher successful response rate when marketing their services than do those with a broad brush approach.

For example Independent Professionals who market their skills to a wider, more general client base are satisfied with a 5 percent client acceptance, but niche marketing enjoys an 80 to 90 percent successful paying client response – that says it all.

Develop your approach

Meet the unique needs in your niche market. The benefits of the services you promise must have one or more special appeals to your market niche.

Consider what you can provide that's new, compelling and highly needed or desired by your prospects? You need to identify the unique requirements of your potential niche audience, and look for ways to tailor your product or service to meet them.

Say the right thing. When marketing to a new market niche, it's important to speak in their language, using their general terms and hot buttons; be prepared to associate with the target group to be seen as one of them and not as an outsider.

It is very important to know and understand your niche market's key issues and have some great solutions with successful case studies for these issues. Ideally you should have had a successful career in your niche market so that your experience and knowledge will give you significant credibility and opportunity.

Always test market. Before involving yourself in any niche market, always research who your competitors are and what they are doing, then determine how you will uniquely position yourself against them:
- Research competitors' adverts, brochures and Websites
- Check out their key selling points,
- Clarify their price points
- Recognise additional service characteristics.

Do not under-price competitors; rather provide additional value for money.

9.4. Client Focus and Commitment

Great Independent Professionals always put their clients first. They commit themselves to providing real benefits that make a difference to those who are paying them good money and expect to continue to provide differentiated products and services.

Competent Independent Professionals truly care about their clients and can effectively become a partner in their client's business.

Dedicated Independent Professionals have a genuine desire to help clients and to maximise their commercial success by providing genuine benefits for their clients, make significant improvements and better the lives of those who hire them.

When Independent Professionals put clients first and drive relentlessly toward producing results for the client, they find the money aspect takes care of itself. Many would-be Independent Professionals fail by not taking this attitude.

An Independent Professional who can't think past getting their fee is someone who is out of focus.

Most people can smell an all-about-the-money person from a mile away. The Independent Professional that delivers a so-so job, and then pockets a hefty fee will soon earn the reputation as someone who delivers the minimum and is in it just for the money.

In summary, the sound Independent Professional will put clients first and be committed to their success. Set your charge high and collect your fee free of guilt – but only if you delivered on the service you promised.

Make that your commitment.

9.5. Relationship Communication

It is very important to keep up a relationship and actively bond with a prospect or client for the potential of further business or for the likelihood of referrals. You must do this in an unintrusive and no-nuisance manner and some ideas on how to do this as a form of a structured communication programme over a 12 month period as follows:

- Formal thanks for their business after winning a contract with them.

- Formal thanks for their business at the end of the contract and at the end of the year in which the work was done (more later).

- Send regular newsletters, seasonal cards, reports, surveys for example.

- Send good quality referrals and introductions.

- Send information about any subject they have a personal interest in e.g. *"Hi John, found this great article on scuba diving in the Great Barrier Reef that you may find interesting when you next go out to Australia."*

- Send your own special offers, or those from your close contacts or Joint Venture partners.

- Invite prospects and clients to seminars and special events; alternatively hold client hospitality events when you provide informative, even entertaining communications with clients. They'll appreciate it and look forward to hearing from you. They are also a great opportunity to encourage clients to bring guests who may be future prospects.

Your main aim is to turn each new client into a proactive walking, talking, word-of-mouth referral machine for you, your products or your services.

9.6. Work Hard but Maintain Perspective

Some people escape the shackles of their regular jobs to become self-employed Independent Professionals, only to become enslaved to themselves. It's easy for many Independent Professionals to become workaholics, the process of getting started with any new business usually requires an enormous amount of work initially and it can often be difficult to pull-back to more normal working hours later.

Another reason some Independent Professionals become workaholics is fear. They think to themselves: *"Now I'm self-employed! The only thing between me and getting my next pay cheque is myself! If I don't keep at it constantly, the work could stop coming and I'd go broke!"*

It's important to be dedicated to your success as an Independent Professional, especially early on, but at some point, you should develop a perspective. Did you really go through the trouble of leaving your old wage-slave job only to become a different kind of higher-paid slave to your own enterprise?

Also, most human beings have important things to be concerned about, such as a spouse, children, maybe a dog and a cat. You can only neglect the personal aspect of your life for so long before things start to crumble. Part of the reason you want to become an Independent Professional is to make more money, and not just because you want to have more money but so you can also have more free time to enjoy that money.

Sure, there are Independent Professionals who love what they do so much, they don't care to take much time off. As the Chinese philosopher Confucius said: *"The man who finds a job he loves will never work another day."* It all depends on you and your personal perspective.

But in general, we can say this: "Show me an Independent Professional who works 18 hours a day, and we'll show you a poor Independent Professional."

So think about it this way: Taking time off does not hurt your business, it helps it! You prevent burn out, you stay sharp, you maintain perspective and you develop an infrastructure that allows you to enjoy life more.

Section 10: Why People Refer You

The list is thankfully quite short but rather powerful.

You have to be professional and committed to the client's success:

- Because they like, respect, appreciate you, your manner, appearance and your professionalism.

- Because you have provided them and their business with one or more benefits and some value and they wish to pass this onto people they know.

- Because you have provided them with referrals and they wish to reciprocate.

- Because they actually want to help you to win new business (sometimes this is very much to their own benefit).

10.1. Types of Referrals

10.1.1. Relationship Referrals

In business-to-business a relationship referral is generally based on two or more people who have developed a good relationship and trust each other and are confident and proactive in regularly recommending each other and their businesses to people they know.

Examples:

- You get excellent service from an accountancy firm and you proactively recommend that business to other businesses you know for their benefit.

Someone asks for your advice or recommendation on where they can get a certain quality/value for money product or service and you recommend businesses you know and have good relationships with.

Such sources of referrals come from a variety of sources including: word of mouth, personal knowledge, goodwill, networking, customers, testimonials, alliance partners, reciprocal gain, professional contacts, special endorsements and loyalty schemes.

These are classed as the best sources of referrals by professional networkers and most referral marketing specialists.

10.1.2. Transaction Based Referrals

These types of referrals happen mostly in Business-to-Business relationships, through Referral Agents or brokers and also affiliate programmes, loyalty schemes and some form of referral activity.

These referrals or introductions are generally provided for some form of reward, for example commission based referrals, celebrity endorsements or incentive rewards.

The referral agent or broker is someone who is generally well connected and well known with a large contact base, sometimes in a niche market; a Mr. Fix It who is proactive in finding contacts for other businesses in return for a commission based fee.

This fee can be either paid for just making the introduction (no matter the result) or as a percentage of the result of a successful lead that turns into business.

A professional referral agent or broker will normally want from you a range of information including: full personal details, endorsements, assurances, guarantees and any outcomes from due diligence before they will refer you.

Normally such agents will also be involved in setting up meetings and introducing prospects and clients to their contacts in a hospitality situation.

10.1.3. Your Referral Marketing Programme

Word of mouth - As a successful professional you will gain continuous word of mouth referrals from peers as well as happy and satisfied customers.

This will happen naturally, but you can greatly increase the rate and success of the referrals you receive with The Professional Referral Programme.

Definition; The Professional Referral Programme is a proactive and structured process that is based on the following steps:

1. – <u>Your Referral Qualities</u> - The quality of your presentation of who you are, what you do, the quality of the services and work you provide, the benefits and value you offer and your past successes.

2. – <u>Referral Mindset</u> – You will always gain referrals from giving referrals FIRST. Always enquire as to the types of contacts that would most interest your clients and contacts and give them useful referrals accordingly.

3. – <u>Motivating your clients and contacts</u> – You want them to pass on the benefits and value you have provided to them to other people they know, hence they will be doing themselves a favour in doing so.

This is simply presenting and reminding your clients of all the positive results of the work you have done for them. This can be presented in your regular activity reports, project feedback and review meetings.

The final project/review meeting is the most important as it is this meeting where you can gain:

– *Testimonials* – When you encourage the client to say anything very positive about your work, reply; *"That is very kind of you to say that about my work for you, would you mind if*

I was to quote you in a testimonial?"
Later send the client a written draft testimonial for their agreement then use it accordingly, sensitively and extensively.

– *Referral leads* – Again when you have encouraged the client to make a positive statement.

You can reply *"That is very kind of you to say that, do you know of anyone who YOU can help who would be interested in receiving the same benefits?"*

When you get referral lead details you can ask *"Will you contact them or would you prefer if I did, if so please be assured that I shall contact them in a very professional manner?"* If the client states they will contact them you can reply *"Can you please advise me when you will be contacting them so I can be prepared for their call?"*

In addition, whether you continue to work for them or not, you need to keep your name in the client's and contact's mind by maintaining your communication programme. This can include:

- Referrals for them,
- Thank you letters,
- Newsletters,
- Reports,
- Surveys,
- Seasonal greetings,
- Annual review meetings,

- Invitations to events and
- Snippets of information that you know will interest them

4. – <u>Create a structured and proactive system</u> – You want to encourage your clients and business contacts to think more about you in a positive manner, thus talking more about you to the people they know.

When you contact them then we suggest you first write to them (email or letter) stating a brief introduction, a case study of the success you have had with the referring client (with client's permission) and their endorsement, then follow-up by phone within 1-2 days.

If the prospect is interested they will often phone the referrer first for confirmation. This process then makes your phone call a <u>very warm call</u> and you should be well received by the prospect.

Note: All quotes are suggestions; please use your own words that you are comfortable with.

<u>10.2. Joint Venture or Alliance Marketing</u>

Depending on the quality of its members and their referral mindset, a Joint Venture or Alliance Marketing group can be one of the most powerful marketing and lead generation strategies you can use as a professional.

A Joint Venture is a group of like-minded top

professionals who work together at a strategic level to gain more business for each other.

When you have to normally promote yourself and your business independently you face various challenges such as lack of time, skills, resources, money, opportunities and perhaps credibility.

When you are a member of a good Joint Venture you can share these marketing challenges with other members and the results that are generated are often greater than those that can be achieved by individual efforts (Synergy).

10.2.1. A Joint Venture Model

– Members who are generally non-competitive, although a group can consist of the same professional types who work in various specialist fields e.g. legal, marketing or finance

– Members deal in similar markets.

– The group has a general theme, for example: Professional, Business Development, Construction or Retail consisting of appropriate types of members.

– The group is very structured with regular meetings, a brand name (sometimes setup as a LLP), a committee structure, an agreed development plan and a bank account.

– All members are VERY REFERRAL MINDED – The group needs this important attitude to succeed.

10.2.2. The Potential Benefits of Joint Venture

There are at least thirteen ways to save on marketing costs:
- Greater return on your investment in time, money, experience,
- Sharing of skills,
- Extended list of contacts,
- Technology,
- Resources,
- Wider market exposure,
- Higher promotional response,
- Better sales results,
- New business contacts,
- New and additional opportunities,
- Extended potential client base,
- Higher company profile,
- Greater credibility for your own business.

Joint Venture Members, the quality of the membership is all important to the success of the group. They all must have a very strong referral mind-set, positive attitude, customer focus, financially stable and a large network of contacts.

All members must continue to consider where they can introduce other members and help as team members in the group's strategic development programme. This co-operative working and sharing of skills is the real strength of a Joint Venture.

Joint Venture Development Plan, this is a 12 month professional marketing plan agreed by all members of the group and will include: the strategies to use, who will be involved, the target aims, costs, promotional methods and resources needed.

Joint Venture Strategies, groups can use all marketing strategies very successfully, the main and most effective is promoting to each member's opted-in network, which will produce high results for negligible cost.

Additionally, members can share a website in the group's brand name and conduct Joint workshops, networking and other events.

Credibility, as a member of a good professional Joint Venture group you gain additional credibility through your association with other members, some of whom may be better known than you.

You Offer Better Value, being associated with a good professional Joint Venture group means you can provide far greater benefits and value over and above your own services (One Stop Shop), which provides you with more successful sales prospects.

New Opportunities, referrals, new business and additional revenue sources can be developed through the other members of the Joint Venture group.

Review Meetings. Using review meetings to gain referrals for members of the group was particularly successful in all Joint Venture groups who used it.

Incentives, you gain greater results from your promotions when members share incentive offers; for example assume you wish to conduct a mail-shot to a niche market with 4 other members who are interested in your promotion; each offers an incentive worth £50. Total incentives are now worth 5 x £50 = £250, which will gain a better response from your prospects, free marketing for your Joint Venture partners and an attractive offer for prospects. A true "WIN-WIN-WIN" solution.

10.2.3. Examples of Joint Venture Marketing

In return for a little commitment, Joint Venture marketing will probably be one of the best opportunities you have for greater success in your business. There may initially be many members coming and going until a good hard core of quality members is established.

I have established some 28 successful Joint Ventures and the results from some of these projects were astonishing, some example case studies are described below:

A Berkshire professional group of nine members wanting to strengthen their image and presence in the area provided two profitable ideas:

Idea 1 – They formally welcomed all new companies into the region with a nice folder and a "Welcome to Berkshire" letter included. The welcome message included offers of help to the company regarding finding local useful contacts and information and also special offers on some of the member's services.

Twelve letters were sent to new companies over an 18 month period, all of which resulted in invitations to the company's premises and some work for various members.

Idea 2 – Also successful was what was called Referral Brokering. All members regularly reminded their own networks that they may be able to find valued contacts for them. If such a request was received, it was passed onto all members, who in turn pass it onto their networks.

If a contact was made then the 2 parties were introduced, sometimes a success finder's fee was charged. This is very powerful and gives great value to all members and their particular networks.

A wedding group of 14 companies, all of whom offered a complete wedding package, used to get most of its additional business through the group's jeweller, who was the first stop for couples getting married to get their engagement and wedding rings. The jeweller sold the package on behalf of other members and greatly increased his own business as well.

A business development group in Oxfordshire, used to hold regular business workshops and seminars, which generated a great deal of new business for all the Joint Venture members concerned. One seasonal hospitality event for customers was particularly successful both for members and for their clients.

Five restaurants in Reading formed a Joint Venture as a Cuisine Group. The restaurants offered different catering themes i.e. Italian, French, Chinese, Tai, Indian and American food.

A voucher system was used where special offer vouchers and a promotional leaflet were issued to all customers to promote all the other member restaurants and their special offers.

Overall average increase in business for the whole group was almost twice the normal business for the time of year.

Eleven DIY Shops in Berkshire, Instead of the 11 separate adverts at an average cost £180 for each shop; they did a whole page for a total cost of £1,200, a cost saving of just over 40% per advertiser.

This saving was in addition to the larger and

more visible marketing message that they could now display on behalf of all the DIY shops in the venture.

The success rate was excellent with some shops reporting treble phone enquiries and double sales.

A Car and a Caravan Retailer conducted a joint promotion each using an award winning product; the UK diesel car of the year and the UK caravan of the year. The car and caravan dealers loaned each other a car and caravan, which were linked up together in the respective showrooms. Both promotions were extremely successful, although no marketing stats are available.

These are just a few of the many examples of properly established Joint Ventures that bring together a mix of consummate professionalism, skills, experience and expertise to collectively benefit each individual business.

Part 2. Business Networking

Introduction

You have worked through how to be the consummate professional, checked with friends and colleagues that the tools and tips are working so now is the time to try it out, make mistakes, learn and improve.

Your Networking Plan

General Principles

Develop a written strategic plan and goals for your networking — make goals obtainable and realistic (e.g. to meet X number of contacts and make Y number of 1-2-1 meetings).

Prepare an event schedule over 3-6 months on a spread sheet, entering all events you know and updating with future events as you find them.

If attending with co-workers, share thoughts, strategy and mental checklist of action items *before* you attend.

Practice your "elevator speech", your professional "Tip of the week" and pertinent questions to ask the people you will meet – and get it all word perfect.

Plan your answer when asked, "What do you do?" example instead of stating "I am a marketing consultant" try instead *"I help companies to maximise their brand awareness and business growth"* or *"I help companies to make more money."*

Be sure to bring a good supply of business cards, referral cards, special offer vouchers and appropriate hand-outs.

Consider the type of people you wish to meet and give thought to who can you introduce to whom from your own contact base to build your favour bank.

Consider and know a bit about some current business topics to discuss, taken from any aspects of business news

Consider any incentives or special offer vouchers to produce and distribute at meetings via marketing tables, personal contacts and announced in elevator speeches.

Bring with you a "Tip of the Week" to engage people and help them do better – but more of this later.

<u>At the reception</u>

Try to arrive early and leave last at events, that way you get better opportunities to talk to people.

Invest in your own professional looking name tag, much better than the yellowing piece of sticky paper you're normally provided with.

Wear your name tag on the right. When shaking hands, a person's eye naturally travels up his or her partner's arm to the shoulder/chest area, they see the name and then the eye travels up to the face.

Ask for an attendance list (if available), if not, create your own.

Ask for the "marketing table" and leave your marketing media there.

Ask for the most influential person(s) in the room at that time, introduce yourself and ask for their help with types of people you are seeking to get in touch with; be sure to thank them afterwards for the introduction.

With people you know, greet them politely and briefly, after all you already know what they do and how you might do business together unless they intend to give you a new introduction.

At the initial handshakes, respect people's personal space — don't crowd them.

Repeat the name of the person when you meet them; it shows you're listening, sounds good to them and helps to embed their name in your already crowded mind.

Be sure you have a brief, effective introduction of yourself — it should take less than 15 seconds, provide your name, areas of interest, and the benefits you deliver, not your job title.

Avoid being loud, be careful on the humour, what makes you smile might make someone else grimace and undermine all the good work you've done thus far.

Avoid smoking before the meeting, take a strong mint if you have a dry mouth.

Be positive and avoid complaining, although there are people who do enjoy a good grumble.

<u>In General</u>

Study other peoples' clothing, their shoes. their blouse, their shirt, their tie — you *can* tell a book by its cover.

Don't sit down at an informal meeting, if you do then never sit at an empty table or next to an empty chair.

Work one-on-one or with small groups, avoid big groups.

Never ever be critical of anyone at the event whether to their face or behind their back to others, always be complimentary.

Be *extra* courteous to the staff — they can be a friend or an enemy, they can support you or scupper you.

Avoid excessive food and drink, even if others are going overboard.

Introductions

Don't be afraid to say to a person or group, "Excuse me—may I join you?"

If you can introduce people to each other do so – and then leave them to it. Ask them later how they got on.

If you ask people for their best prospective contacts and you happen to come across any later at that event, be sure to make the introduction, it makes another friend.

Endorsing other people is great, try to attend the event with a "referral buddy" who is someone you know and you rate very highly and is also very referral minded; the approach is to endorse each other as a mechanism to develop each other's credibility whilst giving information that would not normally be forthcoming face to face (see later in this section for more details).

Focus on introductions and relationships, not selling.

Conversations

Look at, listen and encourage the speaker and resist interrupting.

Spend 95% of the time asking questions about the other person, their business and their immediate needs.

Try to spend most of your conversation without using the words "I", "We", "Our" or "Us".

Repeat in summary what you hear during the course of a conversation — it reflects that you're listening, and it clarifies points made.

Refer back to conversation later in the dialogue — "As you said earlier, ..."

Sometimes it is good to discuss any subject of the contact's interest other than doing business; when you enter a group; listen for three minutes or so and avoid striking up or interrupting the conversation until you're clear about the topic, tone and tensions in the group.

Focus on being interested as opposed to being interesting; try to find two things in common with the other person.

Asking Questions

Have several questions ready in advance that could engage another person, for example: "How would I know if I ran into your ideal client or prospect?"

When introducing someone to someone else, tell a bit about each person to the other, something that might connect them and may be unrelated to business.

Ask open questions – those that require more than a one-word answer, often prefixed with: why, what, when, where, who, how.

Speak clearly and at a medium pace, or a pace to reflect that of the other person

Maintain an approachable expression.

Remembering Names

Repeat the name throughout conversation (judiciously)

One technique is to associate the name with an article of clothing, a feature or a trait; for example wearing a short-sleeved shirt 'short-sleeve' – Steve.

Business Cards

Ask for business cards (rather than offering yours first) and spend some time examining their card, note any honours or qualifications and play them back.

Make notes on the back of a person's business card — "Let me write that down on the back of your card..."

Keep your business cards in an easy-to-reach pocket — pulling them out of your wallet can be clumsy.

Ensure your own cards are a matt finish (at least on the back) so that others can easily write notes and reminders on them.

Body Language

Smile as much as you can, try to look sincere, make and maintain eye contact without staring at people; the norm is to look at a person about 70% of the time if listening, about 50% of the time if you're speaking

Keep a good posture, don't fidget too much and don't get too deep into the other person's space.

Be sensitive to their body language.

The Graceful Exit

You should anticipate that you will spend no more than five to seven minutes with any one individual. After that, you should be prepared to move gracefully on.

When you wish to move on, state how you have enjoyed meeting them and that you both should move on to meet other people: *"Well, I don't want to take up all your time. I'm sure you have other people you want to talk to but I would like to continue our conversation, can we plan to get together? I'll call you next week."*

Be sure to give the other person a get-out if they don't want to continue the conversation you certainly don't want to waste time hunting them down. Although a little persistence can pay dividends, it takes a bit of practice to get the right balance.

<u>Follow-up</u>

Research the most interesting people you have met, send thank-you emails within 24 hours, and make 1-2-1 appointments fairly soon, whilst the gist of the conversation is still fresh and the needs are still current.

At 1-2-1 meetings make note of any contacts wanted and if acceptable and after some relationship development make the introductions.

In follow-up letters, see if you can remember something to ask them to send you. This puts a ball into their court and will help to build a relationship that might be good in the future if not immediately.

Ask if they do not mind receiving future communications from you such as newsletters or white papers.

Stay in touch, send them referrals, appropriate information of interest, newsletters and other items that should be of interest to them.

Types of Meeting

Breakfast meetings

These are absolutely brilliant for early risers, who love a hearty breakfast.

These networking groups are based on membership of the networking organisation and you will be committed to attend a given percentage of meetings on a regular basis.

Additionally, you will be expected to do a one minute presentation about your company and take an active part in the referral session that follows.

You will also be expected to look out for referral opportunities for other members of the group, as other members of the group will be expected to look out for referral opportunities for you.

Open Networking Groups

These events are normally professionally run, structured but without formality, they do not always require you to do a one minute presentation about your business and normally they will not have referral sessions either.

They may incorporate different styles of networking from speed networking to more relaxed round table opportunities, which can be very productive.

These groups are less likely to require membership fees but will often have an attendance fee associated with the event.

Events may be held at different times of the day or in the evening and usually do not provide more than tea/coffee as refreshment.

These events will provide good opportunities to meet a diverse group of business people where you can develop positive business relationships.

<u>People who Lunch</u>

These meetings provide very positive opportunities to meet other business people in a relaxed environment, network informally over lunch and then usually with structured networking afterwards to give the time to explore mutual opportunities.

In this social environment there is very good opportunity to establish and build relationships that will be fruitful in the future. Again these groups are based largely around membership of the organisation and you get best value from attending regularly.

These meetings are held in the middle of the day, after all that's when lunchtime is! The requirement from you is the time to make it work and to recognise the afternoon back in the office will probably be less productive than usual.

Unstructured Networking

These events provide significant numbers of people for you to network with; they are deliberately designed to provide you with the chance to meet a large number of people amongst those who attend.

As a rule they do not require membership, are open and honest about the positive networking opportunities that you can find there and will provide light refreshments only.

These events can be held at any time of the day or in the evening, providing a wide choice of opportunity for business networking.

As a caveat, I personally have found that smaller networking events are more productive, especially if they are in a niche market place.

Specialist Groups

These groups provide very positive networking experiences, whether they are networking for general business or specific professional sectors.

Included in this category are, for example:
- Networking groups for women in business
- Groups run by local Chambers of Commerce
- Small Business organisations and
- Professional bodies.

The culture and dynamics of these networking meetings are different to those mentioned previously. With a far greater probability of a relaxed atmosphere, people who attend can feel less pressured to deliver something and just enjoy the networking process.

These groups meet most frequently in the evening, negating the need to take time out of the working day. For entrepreneurs in particular, that alone can be a significant benefit.

Most of these types of group will be membership based with membership fees varying from as little as £20 per month to anything up to four figures for annual membership.

Business Forums

There are some business forums where a small group of professionals will share ideas on all matter of business subjects, some specialist and some generalist.

As a strategist I personally like these because I can swap ideas on my specialist subject of business development.

Members of such groups find a great deal of benefit from the sharing of ideas and also obtain a good deal of credibility from offering sound advice.

<u>Virtual Networking</u>

A great deal of both social and business networking is now done on line. Despite the fact that people may never meet face-to-face, relationships can be established and business generated.

A good example of this, for business networking, would be LinkedIn whose very large on-line membership stretches literally round the globe as well as LinkedIn there are Facebook, Twitter, Naymz, WeCanDo.Biz, Business-scene and many more beyond the scope of this book.

Tip of the Week

Conducting the "Tip of the Week" idea during the elevator speech session at networking meetings is a very powerful and successful means of getting your attention, credibility and interest from other attendees.

Most people will bore everyone silly with the usual self-promotion of them and their business, if you changed the format and shared some short and useful ideas that may be of use, interest and help to other attendees then you will gain a good deal more attention.

If you happen to know of one or more new attendees at the meeting, you may try using the title "I have a great marketing tip for xxxx" – their business sector.

To gain lasting attention from them it is best to use tip of the week if you can supply everyone with a referral card that presents who you are, what you do and how to get in touch.

Example Tip of the week

For example I may start with "Good evening ladies and gentlemen my name is Vince Golder and I help companies to maximise their word of mouth business."

And continue with a short presentation that last only about a minute, normally less.

"You will find more details about my business on the referral cards I have handed out.

Now I would like to share with you my Referral Marketing Tip of the Week.

How many of you have a Client Charter that you give to your prospects as well as clients?

I have some printed copies of my own Client Charter here. Having such a document is an excellent way to present you and your company as a very professional business – one that has the highest standards in how you think, work and focus on your own clients; and also that you have maximum confidence in your own work.

Having a Client Charter can be a deal breaker and give you a genuine advantage over your competitors. It's a technique that has won me a good deal of business over the years.

I hope you have found this idea of some use, if you wish to discuss this or any other marketing ideas then I look forward to talking to you.

So that's me Vince Golder of Goldnet Referral Marketing with my strap-line "When you focus on your clients, your clients focus on you" Please note I offered some free examples of my own Client Charter, which people are free to modify or copy.

It should also be noted that each copy has my business and contact information if they should wish to follow up.

Part 3. Referral Marketing

Introduction

This part of the book is structured to help improve your sales by using referrals as well as other accepted sales techniques. For some people it will be a refresher, for some a source of new ideas and for others a revelation.

Section A introduces Referral Marketing with 24 tips and techniques to help grow your referral network – and it is estimated that by 2019 more than 70% of worthwhile sales will come by means of referral, so it's worth starting now.

Section B is presented under eight different headings that expand the sales message and provide some format to the sales process and managing that process in a structured and accountable manner

Section C returns to referral marketing and why it works so well. It also puts you in control through the process of givers' gain and developing a mutuality of benefits with all those you come in contact with, whether customers, suppliers, staff, contacts, communities or even family.

Enjoy

Section A - Maximise Your Referrals

There are many ways referral marketing can greatly increase the results of any sales and marketing campaign, either as a standalone strategy, or to complement your existing marketing program.

"It's always more believable to have someone else raving about you, than for you to rave about yourself."

<u>A1. 24 tips</u>

1. - Operate an official referral program that offers customers and business contacts a referral commission on any successful referrals received.

2. - Everybody is looking for an expert in the area they have a need. You should market yourself as that expert – and make sure your referrers know the benefits you can provide for them and their customers.

3. - The number one challenge in marketing is to get your prospect's attention and the second challenge is to get your prospect to trust you and believe your message; this can be helped immensely through a third party referral.

4. - People who give you permission to market to them (through referral) are better prospects, faster buyers and at the best price for you.

5. - People prefer to buy from people they know and trust. Referrals help build that trust.

6. - Recognise and reward performance in your employees (they are also part of the referral process) offer regular opportunities for feedback. Remind them that they and their jobs are important to the overall success of the company. Include certificates, tokens, gifts and incentives for outstanding contributions.

7. - Rank your customers and referrers by how responsive they are to your marketing efforts and then really focus those efforts on the most responsive ones.

8. - Everyone wants to feel special, so create within your business 'VIP' groups, memberships, and special privileges for good referrers and long-time customers.

9. Don't be afraid to use some of your marketing budget to nurture your referrers and a part of your target market with regular contacts and offers.

10. - Use incentives to increase your response results; try to include other incentives from Joint Venture partners to increase the benefit and value of your own incentive at no extra cost to you.

11. - For all customers, contacts, prospects and referrers use a good quality Customer Relationship Management (CRM) system. Note: there are some good free or low cost on-line based CRM systems available.

12 - Plan each marketing campaign thoroughly; referral strategies should be featured in your annual marketing plan and take into account seasonal trends.

13. - Choose target market(s) carefully, try and promote to niche markets.

14. - Use the most up to date and accurate data on contacts and mailing lists that are active in your particular niche.

15. – Always follow-up prospects by phone on smaller mail-shots; you will always achieve better sales results.

16. - Operate professional customer care and communication programs that keep you in regular contact with your customers, so that they remember, appreciate, buy from you and refer you more often.

17. - Use a unique number in each advert or mail-shot via a call tracking service to check which advert or referrer is achieving the best results.

18. - Consider third party endorsers or joint venture partners with large contact bases you can use who would be willing to promote your business on a goodwill, commission, affiliate or reciprocal basis.

19. - It's less expensive to retain existing customers than to find new ones. So remind them with regular contact, they will remember you when they or their friends have a need you can fill.

20. - Thank customers and business contacts for referrals because when you thank people for referring you, your products or your services, this appreciation is generally well received and repeated.

A simple thank you is enough for most people. You can add gifts or cash rewards either to the referrer or to a charity of their choice.

21. - 80% of your referrals will come from 20% of your customers. Get to know who are the best referrers and acknowledge them.

22. - A good way to advertise your product or service is in catalogues and websites with products that are complimentary to yours.

23. - Between 5% and 10% of your customers will buy anything you sell or recommend if you consistently deliver on your promises, exceed their expectations and have frequent, consistent nurturing communication with them.

24. - Send your customers and referrers regular newsletters with valuable content. You maintain yourself as an expert they can trust and return to again and again.

A2. Givers' Gain

The Givers Gain philosophy is a vitally important part of referral marketing and is a concept where businesses work together to help each other bring in new customers.

When people unselfishly focus on others instead of themselves in business networks, and generally, it creates a reputation of one who helps other people and who will, in return, gain from others helping them reciprocally.

Many people do not fully recognise the power of Give to Gain and how it can help their own business, and so are reluctant to practise this process. Give to Gain is a recognised way by professional networkers to get noticed and gain additional clients, grow sales and increase profitable business.

25. - Givers' Gain, when applied by individual business owners professionals and entrepreneurs, is one of the best ways to grow sales, brand awareness, recognition, respect and interest for themselves and their businesses.

26. - There is a spiritual aspect to our lives – when we give we receive – when a business does something good for somebody, that somebody feels good about them! (Ben Cohen, Ben & Jerry's)

A3. Business Networking

One of the most powerful and effective ways to generate referrals is the art of business networking. Unfortunately most business people simply do not network in a structured and strategic way and the most common fault new networkers have is to "power sell" to everyone they meet and then wonder why people will not refer them.

"Business networking is all about meeting and helping people in a strategic and structured manner to build lasting and constructive relationships."

27. - Networking is a fairly well developed science and should be used for first meeting people, building up a great network of like-minded contacts, developing relationships, seeing how you can help others (especially with introductions) and then gaining clients and referrals in return.

28. - The exciting thing about networking is that it can put you in touch with many potential customers or contacts very quickly, but you have to work hard at it to qualify for referrals.

Section B - Generate More Sales

B1. Ensure Employee Engagement

Your employees are an all important part of your marketing model and must be involved where possible. No matter how good your marketing plan, if your employees are not up to standard then you will fail.

"... get the right people on the bus (and the wrong people off the bus) ..." Jim Collins, Good to Great

In order to gain the best performance from customer facing employees:

29. - Know your employees well: on a personal and professional level. What their interests are, their goals, their wants, challenges etc. When people feel better understood and appreciated they relate better, are more motivated, work harder and are more efficient.

30. - Develop employee sales skills: Offer employees opportunities to grow in skills and personal development. Invest in their training, coaching, skills workshops, courses, shadowing and mentoring; increase their responsibility. Encourage them to step up.

31. - Offer employees the authority and support they need: Ensure they have the resources and responsibilities (decision making authority, time, people, budget, training) to do their work effectively.

32. - Have an "Open Door" policy: and encourage employee discussion, input, brain storming and ideas. Reward well for any successful ideas and contributions.

33. - Communicate clearly: Be clear about your expectations of them and what they have to do and the standard that you expect of them. Keep your employees informed about the whole business and particularly about anything that affects their jobs. Lead by example, be the best communicator and be honest and open with them.

34. - Inspire them: Communicate and discuss your team plan and how to get there. Invite their input and participation. Provide opportunities to solve challenges together. Give people the room to be independent and contribute, then let them perform.

35. - Establish SMART goals: (specific, measurable, achievable, realistic, timely). SMART goals are critical to control, delivering quality and successful results.

36. - Be a Great Listener: Attentive listening is a valuable skill for a manager to have, but only if you act on what you have heard.

37. - Treat employees as you would your customers: with the same courtesy, care and manner.

38. - Always have a fast and reliable answering and follow-up service for enquiries.

<u>B2. Strategic Customer Care (SCC)</u>

A SCC Program complements the marketing plan; which details how, what, when and why you will treat and look after your customer at all times.

SCC is designed to maximise the quality of service, care and relationships with your customers and will increase your sales, customer satisfaction, loyalty, profit, referrals and business growth to give you the edge on your competitors.

Development of a SCC plan is easy and inexpensive, but you must back it up with trained and motivated quality staff, and clear company values.

"When you focus on your customers, your customers will focus on you" Vince Golder.

39. - The customers we already have are more important than the customers we only hope to get – so work closely on your existing customers.

40. - Your most valuable asset is your current customer base. Be creative in finding ways to sell more benefits through your products and services more often, to your existing customers.

41. - The more you engage with customers the clearer things become and the easier it is to determine what you should be doing. (John Russell, President, Harley Davidson). But engage customers at a rate that is comfortable with them, do not over engage.

42. - A product or price advantage can be easily duplicated, but a strong customer service culture can't be copied (Jerry Fritz and Vince Golder).

43. - Make a customer, not a sale.
(Katherine Barchetti)

44. - Make your customer your advocate.
(Steve Mullins)

45. - Test each campaign with at least three small trial promotions with different headings, copy, incentives or benefits before committing to the full marketing project.

Then use whichever produces the best results in your main marketing programme.

46. - Set yourself a Business Rating and include:
- The benefits and value you give,
- How you meet the customer's needs,
- The first impression of all aspects of your business,
- The quality of your products/services,
- Your customer service care package, which will include: appreciation, experience,

relationship, trust, credibility, integrity, reliability, quick problem solvers and issue handling.

Rate yourself honestly and improve where necessary.

47. - Ask your customers what they think about you through surveys and customer reviews. This is excellent best practice in the marketing of your business and will benefit you a great deal in providing great branding, testimonials, presentations, sales and referrals.

48. - Send an annual or anniversary letter of appreciation <u>by post</u> to thank them for their business. This is very powerful method of getting customer respect, appreciation, satisfaction and it's amazing very few companies send such letters.

The normal reaction from recipients is a very surprised, positive and appreciative one. Take this opportunity to offer to get together with the customer and to continue to work closely with them and their business through the following year.

49. - Plan your work, produce a marketing plan and then work your plan, remember to keep it simple, base it on achievable aims, include a SWOT analysis and share your marketing plan with all key staff.

A good marketing plan will save your business time and cost whilst increasing profits and business growth.

50. - Test and monitor your marketing strategies a point at a time before full financial and operational commitment. Have various versions of adverts, mailers, sales letters, emails etc. Conduct small promotions with different incentives/offers and see which version achieves the best response, then use it accordingly. In due course, this will save you time, costs and achieve greater marketing results.

B3. Grow business through your customers

Most companies only see one or two means to develop revenue from existing customers – in reality there are at least three revenue opportunities, with continuous growth gained through structured referrals (the Snowball Effect). The three top opportunities are:
- 1. Gain on-going sales from each customer
- 2. Increase on-going sales from each customer (up-sell or cross-sell)
- 3. Actively obtain additional business from new customers referred by existing customers (this is becoming increasingly important).

51. - Understanding Your Customers is the key to giving them the best service and care. And you must deliver what you promise. Great customer care involves getting to know your customers so well that you can anticipate their needs and exceed their expectations.

52. - Get to know your customers and what they want by continual dialogue using a structured follow-up programme: at point of sale and after sale; this can be prompted by using customer surveys, conversation at hospitality meetings or events and by setting up a Customer Advisory Board (CAB). The CAB is more normal with Business-to-Business relationships.

53. - Focus on customer intelligence to understand your customers, their needs, wants and issues in order to gain their appreciation, respect, satisfaction and loyalty and manage product and service development exactly to customer's needs.

54. - Always consider up-selling to your own customers first, before promotion to cold prospects.

55. - Include high quality testimonials in all your marketing media, with name and if possible a picture of the endorser.

56. - You and your staff need to be attentive to the customers whenever you are in contact with them and also conduct regular customer surveys and reviews to maximise customers' referral sales potential.

B4. Differentiate your Offering

Being ordinary is not an option – you need to be special to get noticed.

"Marketing is a battle of perception. No matter how good you are, your prospect's perception of you is always their reality."

57. - In the world of small business, you don't just have to be better than your competition, you also have to be different and then let people know about it.

58. - Customers buy based on emotions and then justify their purchase based on logic, so remember to include both elements in your marketing message.

59. - Successful sales result from a combination of multiple marketing efforts, programs, and media.

60. The more you tell, the more you sell. Prospects are tired of worn out old sales pitches...they want to be educated rather than sold.

61. - People buy more while they're in the buying mood – which is right after they have made their purchase.

62. - Your customers will tell you which marketing medium to use if you observe what they watch, where they spend their time, and what they listen to.

63. - Too many choices confuse people and confused minds generally say 'no'. Reduce the amount of options you give somebody.

64. - Marketing budgets start by knowing the lifetime cash value of new customers and producing a good marketing plan.

65. - People buy based on value and value is defined as the perception of benefits divided by price. If price goes up and the perceived benefits stay the same, the value goes down...and vice versa.

66. - The closer your marketing message is to the wants and desires of your market, the higher your response rate will be.

67. - Never run down the competition.

B5. Campaign Tactics

68. - Prospects need multiple exposures to your marketing message. 81% of all sales are made on or after the fifth contact with your prospect.

69. - People are more motivated to action by the avoidance of pain than by the promise of gain.

70. - The key to creating an irresistible offer is to build value through benefits and premiums rather than through creative price discounting.

71. - The secret to generating fresh marketing ideas is to observe successful marketing strategies from other industries and adapt them to yours.

72. - Never let a day go by without doing something proactive to generate future business.

73. - Target your prospect with surgical precision. You need to know their demographics, psychographics, geographics, hobbies and occupation.

74. – You may be wasting your marketing budget on general advertising so carefully advertise to your specific, clearly defined target market.

75. - Identify the market with the biggest pain or problem and then build a campaign around how your product or service can solve their problem.

76. - You need to communicate and make offers on a regular basis so that you will always be in the forefront of your customers mind.

77. - Review and analyse your customer information and you will find ways to better talk to the needs of your less responsive customers.

78. - Occasionally ask your customers what other products or services they would buy from you and then find a way to meet their needs.

79. - You will obtain more leads if you use multiple steps in guiding your prospect to a final sale. If it's slow, easy and low risk, they will be herded down the golden path.

80. - See what your competitors are doing and sift the 'pearls' that can be applied to your marketing strategies.

81. - Be willing to ask your prospects about their needs and wants so you can more exactly meet those needs and increase your sales.

82. - Most sales are concluded on the 4th or 5th attempt of contact with cold prospects, don't be afraid to be be persistent – ***be repetitive***.

There was a story running some years ago as to why the Japanese were so successful getting into Europe and the statistic was that a UK sales person would take three rejections and then go elsewhere, an American would take four rejections but the Japanese would take twenty one rejections before giving up – which led to such an amazing record of success.

83. - Use a visitor capture facility on your website that provides an attractive free offer in return for visitors' names and email addresses.

84. - Always be prepared to resend mail.

85. - A phone call follow-up greatly increases results. Follow-up prospects by phone on all targeted promotions, you will always gain better results. Many prospects will tell you that they did not receive your mail (due mainly to gate-keeper's actions), so make sure the promotion-shot is designed for best presentation and retention.

86. - Under promise and over deliver to impress your customer and gain additional goodwill. It also gives you some grace in case of any unforeseen difficulties.

B6. Niche Marketing

Narrow your focus, maximise your potential.

One of the fastest ways to increase response in selling, word of mouth referrals and customer loyalty is to identify a very narrowly focused market segment, understand it well, utilise it, achieve dominance and fill that gap with your products or services.

When you operate in a clearly defined niche market which has highly specific needs, and you offer a product or service to that market in a way that no one or few others are doing, you can become a market leader in that area.

87. - **As an expert** in your niche, identify how the services you provide surpass your competitor's services – and tell people.

88. - **Concentrate your fire-power**; think of the old adage: "A fox that chases too many rabbits will always go hungry." Mike English.

89. - **Always provide more** than you promised, and you will find your customers will return again and again.

90. - **Capitalise on any unique aspect** or feature of your product or service and you'll easily outsell your competition.

91. - **It's easier to market your product** as specialised and ask a higher price rather than take a generic approach and miss your target market.

92. - Don't guess or presume what you think your prospect should want. Use fact based research to find out what they want and then provide that to them.

93. - Some of the best headlines and creative marketing copy are recycled from the successful ideas of others. Smart marketers reuse good ideas, they don't reinvent the marketing wheel.

94. - To remain competitive businesses must frequently look at new ways to market or re-package their products and services to keep them new and interesting.

95. - Match the copy content and message to your niche market: e.g. *"The best marketing solution for accountants"* if you are promoting to accountants.

96. - Use expert advice, services and facilities where needed; for example with planning, copy writing, SEO or strategy. Such expert advice will save you costs, time and risk whilst letting you improve results, grow profits, increase efficiency and become more effective.

97. - Use words that gain interest and sell. There are words you must include in all of your marketing media and there are ones you must always avoid; use a professional copy writer for best results.

B7. Value for Money (VFM)

It is unwise to pay too much. But it is worse to pay too little. When you pay too much, you lose a little money; that is all. When you pay too little, you sometimes lose everything because the product or service you bought is incapable of doing what it was bought to do. The common law of business prohibits paying a little and getting a lot. It can't be done.

If you deal with the lowest bidder, it is well to add something for the risk you run. And if you do that, ask if you would then have had enough to pay for something better or more appropriate.
"There is hardly anything in this world that someone can't make a little worse and sell a little cheaper – and people who consider price alone are this man's lawful prey" John Ruskin.

98. - To promote the best VFM in your products and services, include the following terms:

- **Economy** – careful use of resources saves expense, time or effort.
- **Efficiency** – the same level of service delivered for less cost, time or effort.
- **Effectiveness** – a better standard of service or getting a better return for the same expense, time or effort.
- **Variety** – a greater range of benefits and value than originally anticipated.

99. - People want to be able to justify the emotional purchase they are going to make. Showing them the amount of money they save over a year, or their return on investment, is a powerful tool to help them to buy.

100. - Use Guarantees as a unique part of your selling proposition and irresistible offer. Multiple guarantees work better than a single guarantee, and be sure to make one of the guarantees unconditional.

<u>B8. Some sales truisms</u>

101. - The more you lower the risk of doing business with you, the higher your sales will grow.

102. - Create a marketing message that is easily repeated and lends credibility to the benefits of your product or service. The world is full of sceptics; create a message that reduces their risks and concerns.

103. - Identify your prospects biggest, ugliest problem and then get them all worked up about the problem. When you show how your product or service solves that problem, the sales begin to flow.

104. - The best headlines can be long and full of intense copy that will keep your prospect reading for more – although you can create short headlines that grab your prospects attention.

105. - The dual purchase 'trick' will increase sales and profits. To accomplish this sales approach you need to have multiple products or smaller trial versions of your product to up-sell these products to your prospect.

106. - When you successfully create a compelling advert and begin getting responses, it is critical that you follow up quickly to close the sale.

107. - A successful business has some way to capture the names of not only people who make purchases, but those who make enquires as well.

108. - Don't make the mistake of holding too many sales. If you do, your customers will wait for a sale rather than buy now at the regular price.

109. - While your business is young, concentrate on selling your specific product; you can add related products as your business matures.

110. - Newsletters are a great way to have continued contact with your customers and show that you are a solid business that will be around a long time.

111. - Don't think all you need to know about marketing can be found in books. It's to your benefit to attend marketing seminars and events to keep abreast of new trends and ideas.

112. - If you create new products on a regular basis, a great way to market these is to invite your regular customers to preview and evaluate a sample. Your evaluation sheets will be a great source in determining who needs sales follow up and you should also get some insights of how to improve your product.

113. - When launching a new marketing campaign, see if you can time your launch around a special event, season or holiday. Tying this in with an event will help name recognition and keep the new campaign more memorable.

114. - Three is the magic number when creating visuals in marketing. Using three different fonts, three different colours, in three different groupings will keep your message focused and memorable.

115. - Stay on top of your image. You don't need to change your brand image to keep your image fresh. However, you should periodically look at the image you are portraying and be sure it's in line with your marketing strategy.

116. - Always monitor your results from each promotion for future reference and to calculate the ROI from your marketing.

Section C. - More Referral Marketing

Referral Marketing is a proactive, strategic, structured and systematic process that maximises word of mouth referrals from customers and business contacts.

Referral Marketing incorporates the best presentation of you, your company and your products and services, plus your customer service and experience; consequently customers talk more enthusiastically about the benefits and value you provide to people that they know.

C1. The Power of Referral Marketing

- Referral marketing is recognised as the most cost effective means of lead generation.

- There are far more benefits associated with referral marketing than any other form of marketing.

- A referred prospect comes to you without having to make a phone call, place an advert or send direct mail. They are easier to close and at the most profitable price for you.

- Referred customers are more loyal and great advocates for your business and importantly they become additional sources of referrals for your future business growth. These referrals can increase progressively by the snowball effect.

- Most businesses only get 40% of the word of mouth referrals they should get, structured referral marketing should at least double their word of mouth business.

117. - Customers can be ambassadors too; you can train them to be part of your sales team using selected tips and procedures from this book.

118.- Have a Referral Mindset which focuses on you referring other people FIRST. This should also apply to your staff as well. Some of the best referrals I have had have come from giving referrals first and getting some back reciprocally.

119. - Referral value is recognising that every customer is important, but some may have a greater referral value to you than others due perhaps to their referral mindset, or they are very well respected with high credibility and have a large network of contacts.

120. - Learn to recognise which of your customers have high referral value, so that you can focus your energy on those people and bolster your referral effort.

121. - Never freeze out those customers with low referral value, remember that people's circumstances change. A low referral value business contact or customer today may be elected president of a business association with tens of thousands of members tomorrow!

122. - Never forget a contact and they won't forget you.

123. - Continually ask yourself your customers and your referrers why should people refer you to do business with you and your company.

Be honest, learn and employ the solutions to the questions you ask in all your sales and marketing media.

124. - Always ask for referrals even though most people are reluctant to ask customers for referrals, mainly because of the fear of rejection which is unfounded.

One approach is to ask *"Who do you know who can be helped with the same benefits?"* which then makes it sound like it's their idea. The worst that can happen is that they'll refuse to participate.

125. - Always take notes they may identify future opportunities as well as highlighting areas to develop.

126. - Test, monitor and improve employees' customer skills because customer skills are essential to produce higher sales, enhance customer experience, increase loyalty, and deliver a continual supply of referrals.

The company should be truly customer and employee focused, with strong company values and should treat their employees as they would their customers.

127. - Train your customers to be your ambassadors, educate them on the benefits and value you give, train them how to refer you – and reward them for doing so.
You will end up with a very powerful sales force that could easily exceed the performance of any professional sales team, thus saving your business a great deal of money and resources.

C2. Why Referral Marketing Works

There have been many surveys conducted on what is the most cost effective means of lead generation and all of the surveys concluded that word of mouth was the clear winner in that:

- 92% of consumers worldwide trust recommendations more from friends and family than any other form of advertising.

- 82% of US consumers are influenced by their friends' social media posts.

- 26% of the population influence the purchasing activities of the other 74%.

Source: – The Word of Mouth Marketing Association (WOMMA).
http://www.wommapedia.org/

"Shoppers are most interested in hearing from their peers about products, retailers, and past shopping experiences. Consumers say that word of mouth is still the number one influencer in their apparel (34.3%) and electronics (44.4%) purchases."

Source: - Retail Advertising and Marketing Association/ BIGresearch.

"Recommendations from consumers (78%) are the most trusted form of advertising out there, along with consumer opinions posted online (61%)".

Source: - Nielsen Online Global Consumer study.

"Word-of-mouth is one of the most credible forms of advertising because people who don't stand to gain personally by promoting something put their reputations on the line every time they make a recommendation".

Source: - Entrepreneur Media.

"Among the 17 million adults who found a new primary care physician in the past year, half relied on recommendations from friends and relatives, and more than one in four used such recommendations as their only information"

Source: - HSC 2007 Health Tracking Household Survey.

"A recent survey of subscribers to the American Laundry News Wire determined that word of mouth is the most popular tool for marketing laundry services"

Source: - http://www.prestigecorp.com/News

"61% of influencers turn to Word of Mouth for making shopping and retail purchase decisions."

Source: - Keller Fay Group.

"Word of Mouth sells cars. Automotive consumers may come from all walks of life, but what they drive identifies them. They share in a common passion, as well as the need to engage with other like-minded drivers, for support, to seek advice, express themselves, share experiences, and even show off"

Source: http://www.beaffinitive.com.

128. - Use a Strategic Customer Care (SCC) program as a core base to win your customers over. Invest 80% of your marketing commitment and budget on your SCC program.

129. - Develop a customer communication and referral program that will help customers educate others about your business and an incentive program to reward referrals.

130. - Yellow Pages' strap-line is *"Let your Fingers do the Walking"* the one for referral marketing is; **"Let Your Customers do the Talking".**

In Conclusion

Thank you for your time.

I am confident that you will find these marketing ideas to be useful to you and your business.

As I tell my customers – all great ideas are totally useless until you put them into action, then once you commit to a structured marketing plan you will find your ideas become realistic, productive and successful.

If you would like to add ideas please get in touch, you will be acknowledged in future publications if they are used.

If you like this pocket book please tell others; if not, please tell me.

And, here's to your future success.

Vince Golder

Services

Consultancy

Sales Development

Training

Public speaking

Publishing

Executive Coaching

To contact Vince Golder:

- Phone: 44/7799348642

- Email: vgolder@hotmail.com

About the Contributors

Vince Golder joined the RAF as an apprentice at 16 and served for 20 years, on leaving the RAF he established Goldnet Referral Marketing Ltd. which has been active for over thirty years providing specialist services on referral and Joint Venture marketing through consultancy, training, public speaking and publishing. Vince has created a low cost and productive solution for long-term growth using a proven and powerful referral marketing programme for all types and sizes of companies in all industries.

This referral marketing programme is very dependent on businesses and individuals presenting and working in a consummate professional manner. It is this professional model that is the core of this book.

Testimonial: *"The benefits that we got from Vince's work have been immense. especially in changing in the professional mindset of our team to encourage word of mouth referrals and the way that we have been able to help our clients get more business as well will help build the reputation of our practice for years to come."*
Malcolm Palmer, MD of Accountants for Growth Solutions, Kent

Vince is an internationally acknowledged expert in referral marketing, recognised by top marketing gurus such as:

- Richard Denny, the famous international business development expert and bestselling author.
- Ivan Meisner, the founder of BNI the world's largest business network.
- Brian Smith the inventor of AirMiles and many other business schemes.

Steve Mullins developed his management perspective originally in major blue-chip companies and latterly in a self-employed role.

He has been recognised as one of the best for Marketing Strategy and Business Planning in the south-east of England.

He is director of Ascot Associates Ltd

We hope you will gain a great deal of benefit and value from this book that will contribute to your continued success. The ideas we have shared with you are simple, low cost and easy to implement, the only thing left to do is to commit to them and to use them.

Terms of Use and Disclaimers

1. You must not:

1.a Publish, republish, sell, license, sub-license, rent, transfer, broadcast, distribute or redistribute this publication or any part of this publication by any means whether electronic or physical.

1.b Edit, modify, adapt or alter this publication or any part of this publication.

1.c Use this publication or any part of this publication in any way that is unlawful or in breach of any person's legal rights under any applicable law, or in any way that is offensive, indecent, discriminatory or otherwise objectionable.

1.d Use this publication, or any part of this publication to compete with us, or for any other competitive commercial purpose.

1.e Delete, obscure or remove any copyright notices and other proprietary notices.

2. This is not advice

2.a This publication contains information and ideas about ways to improve your business and personal circumstances; this information is not advice and should not be treated as such.

2.b You must not rely on the information in this publication as an alternative to legal or professional advice from an appropriately qualified practitioner.

2.c You should not delay seeking legal advice, disregard legal advice, commence or discontinue any legal action because of information in this publication.

3. Fitness for purpose

3.a Whilst Vince Golder, Steve Mullins and Ascot Associates Ltd. have endeavoured to ensure that all information is correct, neither Vince Golder, Steve Mullins nor Ascot Associates Ltd. can warrant or represent its completeness or accuracy, or fitness for purpose when used by a third party.

3.b Vince Golder, Steve Mullins and Ascot Associates Ltd. do not warrant or represent that the use of this publication will lead to any particular outcome or result.

In particular there is no guarantee that by using this publication you will obtain additional business or become personally more successful.

4. Limitations and exclusions of liability

4.a Vince Golder, Steve Mullins and Ascot Associates Ltd. will not be liable for any damages, losses or consequential losses arising out of any action, event, or as a result of any action or event, occurring from your using the material in this publication.

5. Governing law

5.a This notice shall be governed by, and construed in accordance with, English law.

Other Related Publications

Books

The Story of Cash Flow
ISBN 978-0-9576340-2-2

Probably the world's first fairy story about business and a guide for the fledgling entrepreneur – how you might get tripped up and what to look out for

How To Market Yourself In A Week
ISBN 978-0-9576340-3-9

The book is written from personal experience of being fired quite a few times and also from successfully outplacing others. It takes you through a series of steps to get a new job – or even to help gain promotion.

Articles

Referral Marketing

How to get your customers to sell for you (part three of this pocket book).
By Vince Golder.

How Good is My Glue?

Non-Financial Due Diligence, taking a look behind the numbers to check compatibility at merger or takeover.
By Steve Mullins.

How Near is My Cliff Edge?

Five easy questions with ten searching answers that takes you to the foundation of your business by inviting you to critically ask what your business really does and how do you go about it.
By Steve Mullins.

All available on Kindle

Papers

Ethical Crisis Management
ISSN 1741-5187

Explores how any decision point pushed back far enough results in what is seen as a good outcome.

by Steve Mullins

Published by: The International Journal of Management and Decision Making, Volume 6, Nos. 3 and 4, 2005, pp.372-381; available only from the publisher.

©Ascot Associates Ltd.

If you like this pocket book and think it will help other people you know, then

Please refer it for your mutual benefit

If you don't like this book, tell us and we can do something about it in the next edition.

©Vince Golder and Steve Mullins 2015
All rights reserved

www.ingramcontent.com/pod-product-compliance
Lightning Source LLC
Chambersburg PA
CBHW031425210526
45464CB00005B/2050